Advance Praise

"*Questions for Water* offers engagement with poems that fearlessly embrace many of the painful realities of our lives today — poems that remind us that trying to stay safe in this world is about as impossible as holding onto a fistful of water. These are poems about the new "vocabulary of america" that requires us to choose to confront our very real fears. They are poems that challenge us to accept the radical ambiguity that now hovers over most everything. While these poems do not flinch from the fact that our world is a dark place, they invite us to seek the light that glows through "the blue green water" of our lives; a quest that is encouraged by our "unending length of longing." "We must each," Crawford writes, find our own compass, and use "the elements available....to make of life what we will / what we can"".

> — Michael Glaser, former Maryland Poet Laureate, author and editor of more than ten volumes of poetry, professor emeritus St. Mary's College of Maryland

"Through a clear, consistent and reflective voice, using organic lines and structures, Virginia Crawford's poems in *Questions for Water* search life's full range of moods, experiences and personal histories with a sense of urgency that our tumultuous daily lives insist upon. In a kind of domino effect, one poem seems to set the next one naturally down, each "held together by an invisible force//their single movement/a form of human union". Expressive and meditative, quiet and inclusive, these inquisitive poems grope for answers in the social landscapes and universal particulars of our twenty-first century lives."

> — Edgar Silex, author of *Through All the Displacements, and Acts of Love*

"Crawford's debut book is a map for our present-day society with its challenges and dangers to home and well-being. These are serious issues for poetry, but intelligence and compassion are the perfect combination to serve reality, then to salvage it. Social action takes many forms and when commentary becomes art we have a journey for change. As pervasive as societal conditions are, the poem reinforces what is best in us — language from the heart. Crawford has the gift of creating experience and then clarifying. She talks of fear but rewards it with light. This is what I see, page after page, an emotional response which calms us, words said thoughtfully, made beautiful."

— Grace Cavalieri, Maryland Poet Laureate

questions for water

virginia crawford

Apprentice
House Press
Loyola University Maryland

First Edition

Paperback ISBN: 978-1-62720-325-8
Ebook ISBN: 978-1-62720-326-5

Printed in the United States of America

Design: Katie McDonnell
Promotion Plan: Rosie DiTaranto
Managing Editor: Danielle Como

Author photo by Sam Schmidt

Published by Apprentice House Press

Apprentice House Press
Loyola University Maryland
4501 N. Charles Street
Baltimore, MD 21210
410.617.5265
www.ApprenticeHouse.com
info@ApprenticeHouse.com

Thanks to Sam and Sherry for sharing so much of their hearts and minds and poetry, and thanks to Nef'fahtiti for her invitation, and to Donna for her art that inspired the title poem.

Contents

everything is a present

soup and war

sorting socks

you're 18 just graduated from high school
in two days you will leave your childhood
the house you grew up in the room you arranged and rearranged
me
i'm sorting socks as if my life depends on it

i've taken all your single socks
pulled more from my bottom drawer
and spread them black then white
solid colors then patterns
such abundance i should be optimistic
how easily things become lost

recently this memory replays
the pair of us me walking you through the neighborhood
me kissing the top of your head
i'm showing you rose and dog and tree
whispering their spanish and italian siblings
into your tiny ear hoping imagining you
creating sets things that belong together

i find a pair fold one mouth securely over its mate
ask if it's one you want in the suitcase
yesterday i threw you a dirty pair you had left in the living room
told you to put it in with the rest
and today i find only one
pale blue with a pattern stitched in

both washer and dryer empty
not behind them or fallen under the sofa
i worry it's a pair you want to take with you
i worry about things finding their mates
finding their way
then
their way back

the white shirt

this morning my son wore a clean white shirt to school
when i saw it all i could do was hope
it stays white all day

he tells me how after
the announcement over the intercom
his teacher locked the door turned off the lights
told everyone to remain seated silent
my son realized he was closest to the door

without mentioning fear he explained
how he'd planned if someone shot in the door
to shield himself with his binder
and rush them

he heard the sirens
arriving in two large waves
a few minutes between them
the loud reports of what he later learned
were lockers being slammed shut

the email the school sent that afternoon
explained there was talk of a gun
that the police were called and did
a thorough sweep
no gun was found

i keep thinking of him in that seat
his fourteen year old heart pumping with adrenaline

this morning i got up early to hug him
i made coffee asked him to take out the trash
pretending it was just thursday
as he left for school
he turned and looked me in the eye
he was pretending too

baltimore

he approaches my car
stopped at a red light
it's winter
his hands bare
red cracked swollen
might bleed at any moment

i place an orange
in his destroyed hand
then wishing him luck
as i do each time
i look up

he's young
hard to tell beneath
his experience
his tears

this young man
stands
in the road
holding an orange
crying

he says between sobs
hot food
i only want
hot food

after jury selection

i make dinner
eat with my son talk with my daughter
after she returns from her lesson
in my own home
my own bed with my husband his arm draped over me
our dog

and i can't sleep

i'm exhausted drunk
from trying to forget
from my potential to ignore

a trial starts tomorrow
for that young man in baltimore
whose name i heard several times
but still could not repeat for you
accused of illegally possessing a firearm
on a particular night last august
on a particular street i don't know

the unfamiliar syllables of his name
the geography of another baltimore

our choices not just the number
the kinds of choices
each a web catching what
degrees home debt
guns gangs prison

so many assumptions

this trim man in his twenties wears a pale green shirt
tie trousers dress shoes
he sits calm and attentive at the defense table
reading over the papers commenting to his lawyer
approaching the bench when requested
or given permission
he also wears many tattoos a kind of map of himself

these are all i know of him
it's impossible to know what his family would say of him
if he has siblings or someone like a father
but he is some mother's son

all day long the weight grows
pursues me down the high-ceilinged halls of the court house
while waiting for my number to be called
looking up the larger than life portraits all white men
the weight grows
even as i scuttle along the sidewalk at dusk
trying to find the car
it has been growing every day of my life
his life
hundreds of years

all day long all i wanted
was to escape my city's
my country's dark mirror

here i am not sleeping

each breath each generation
heavier with loss
none of us escape
that chain of history
from africa from europe
to this shore
this city

all of us weighted
with everything we have
and have not become

every time i hear a siren

i beg the universe
for them not to be going to my children's schools
to any school

this morning i took her in late
heard them racing
closer as i turned out of the lot

i pushed myself to continue to work
they could be going anywhere
it's going to be a normal day

all morning i teetered
into away from tears
in my not knowing

they were headed
to a school half a mile away
this time no students were shot

can you imagine first period
hearing that sound inside your school
the lockdown signal
not knowing if you would leave school alive
or in a body bag

this afternoon the email
a student's family member
shot a special education teacher
school security contained
the shooter almost immediately
teacher in stable condition

no back story
could make this make sense

consider what it would take for this to be your choice
how do students walk through the buildings
where their teachers and friends have been shot
how has this become
the vocabulary of america
how do i send my children to school
when i cannot be sure
they will survive the day
how can i protect them
from what they are learning
from the ways we are living
and dying

thoughts on making soup and war

for nef'fahtiti and imani

the potatoes brown and
beautiful and cool wait
in line beside my cutting board

i slice each into chunks then
slide them so many
half moons into a boiling pot

the body of an onion
beneath my palm this raw
material for cutting and using

luminous layers of white
the scent familiar irritating
america has made me soft

my trash can overflows
with food i cannot eat
quickly enough while someone

down the street goes hungry
too many times i stop
at a red light where a veteran lives

his warped cardboard sign held high
another flag he carries now and i do not
have an apple a bed

a dollar bill to give him
how how do we sleep
through war

like that day we saw the pairs
of boots lined up one pair
for each soldier lost

so far each perfectly formed
to the feet that used to sweat in them
an army of ghosts called to attention

across the perfect grass
then our friend said
her middle son had signed up

her face her heart all of her
fell open what used to shine there now
dark with love and worry i held her

as we cried and she said *don't*
take my baby don't send my baby
to iraq she said it over and over

and we cried our whole bodies
shaking for our sons

going to bed after pbs

i'm on my sofa wearing a satin nightgown
white and pink learning about the child
sex trade in thailand the program
describes in this particular region almost
complete unemployment the non-existence
of schools the residents' futile attempts
to grow their own food the daily pressure
to sell their daughters and i'd have to agree
escape seems impossible
but i tell myself surely
i'd sell myself or starve before i'd
sell my girl sleeping in the next
room before i'd let her brother
think she's something to be sold
how do you wear clothes and live
in a house built with your girl's
dignity and how do parents survive
that silent black river neither can speak of
now flooding their homes and what about
the men who pay to spend a month
with a virgin perhaps nine years old
a nine-year-old virgin and the people
who run the hotels and restaurants
who know the people who know
people know nine-year-olds are being sold
then the girls the girls what do they do
with their minds when those men
open their pants crush them against

a bed or floor where are they when
those men are inside them when sweat
drips onto their faces how do they leave
those hotel rooms how
will they find home

american mom

after a us missile kills an iranian leader
we are told to expect retaliation

your brother is thankful he's two
years shy of eighteen i stop myself
from saying wars last many years
instead i look at the map
for the place our friends mentioned
in canada if it comes to that

of course the route goes through
that most beloved target
new york city

where you my daughter happen to be
visiting a friend
not knowing if i should
if i will alarm you or
if you will then ignore
i text first ask
how you're doing
working up to no one knows where
or when but iran says it's going to
start killing americans
please consider some places
that might be safe if something happens

just like that
it's eighteen years ago
you were six months old

a student ran in saying
a plane hit a tower
the radio told us a second tower
authorities considering shutting down 95
which i used between your sitter's and the college
i raced to get you
then home i held you on the sofa
in front of the tv
where the planes flew
through that bright blue tuesday sky
into the towers
again and again and again

i text and ask
for any addresses of friends
you might go to
if something happens nearby
and i have to explain
i'm on the sofa
remembering everything
covered in ash   humans
covered in ash humans
running anywhere away
news that phones were jammed
all the people who couldn't find their people

then papers posted to walls often with pictures
have you seen
then lists and lists of names

i never want to not be able to find you
if i have addresses if i can't reach you
hopefully i could see on a map that you are
staying safely blocks and blocks and miles away
from where it happened

you send your friend's address
i darn your wool sweater in my lap

traveling south in a snowstorm

as my son and i leave northern vermont
everyone saying it will be okay once you're on the highway
even after someone gets stuck at the top of the driveway
even after their rescuer slides into the ditch
i pray no one's coming as we
continue up the hill turn
onto the road slushy with snow and ice

small as i am i hunch over the wheel
trying to see through crystals multiplying across the windshield
every few moments a thin stream
of blue fluid a flash of wipers
i wonder how much fluid there is
how long crystals will try to occupy the windshield
i focus on the tracks made by the car ahead of us

in the graphic novel my son reads a superhero
teleports to mars to escape humanity
many times i have wished for such power

snow and ice continue to fall on this
rural unlit highway no way
to delineate lanes or shoulder even
if i could see the road's surface

our wheels spin and slide
stomach hands mind
turn into the slide

the dashboard indicates it is twenty-six degrees
the windshield crystalizes again
i almost give up

to fear my desire for our bodies to remain unharmed
but i've already reserved a room for the night
it is twenty-eight degrees outside

i persist at the raging pace of forty miles an hour
my son sleeps an hour two
after six hours snow and ice are rain
in connecticut it is thirty-three then thirty-four degrees

at breakfast
we each make a waffle
pour the batter close the irons
red numbers count down

we face the tv news

american jews are being attacked
european jews are being attacked
in australia there's a town dark two hours after sunrise
smoke so thick all is darkness maybe
midnight without stars
in another town the air appears to be dyed red

there will be no fireworks over most of australia this new year's
then video kangaroos bounding across brown land
each body's singular exertion
the ancient brain commanding all effort and energy
toward its intention to survive

their flight jolts me
seeing these large mammals
the immediacy of desperation
the way we have become far too
accepting of the desperation around us

in my son's book after the hero asserts
every human being is their own thermodynamic miracle
this truth a momentary refuge to me
the hero decides to interrupt
the annihilation of humanity
that has already begun
the illustrations heaps of bodies
so much blood
a poster advertising the pale rider
playing with kristallnacht
i suck in my breath

we are fifty miles from where last night
someone broke
into a rabbi's home
into the celebration of the seventh night
wielding a machete

back on the road i am momentarily
comforted by the relative normalcy of the new jersey turnpike
access to bathrooms food running water and soap
this rest stop dedicated to edison

who said our biggest mistake is giving up
in the bathroom almost always being cleaned by hispanic women
signs asking estas buscas una salida
are you looking for a way out

given all these truths
all the confusion and blood and miracles
all the horrors our children are inheriting
i have no idea what to say to my son
i can't say anything if i open my mouth

all i can do
is be there silent sad
my hand on my son's shoulder

questions for water

questions for water

it's a blue green white day
i tell my teenage daughter as we drive
trying to make conversation
hoping to hear what she thinks

blue sky green world white clouds
i remind myself to be thankful

quiet or music
whisper and roar
it's everywhere
the sound of the oarsman
a heartbeat
the child's cry

how is the sea green here blue there
what do you call that place where they mix

in the foreground mountains
earth vines
a trap called memory
barbed wire hoops to jump through

how do you hold a fistful of water
keep your child your child
how do you hold
a fistful of blue green blue
light streaming between your fingers

my daughter is an island
too far for me to swim

she's made of sand constantly shifting
becoming

i wait on a different shore
i wait beside my mountain

how did we get here
which coast did we sail from

blue green blue
sometimes ripples of sun

the day we took the german exchange students to the beach
parked and walked through the cool forest
came back with fossils in our pockets
shark teeth grey and white
we were not far from
where my grandmother grew up
where work is crabbing picking
she eventually moved to baltimore
sold vegetables to immigrants

blue and green
mixed
nothing on its own
even water h 2 and o
everything mixed
sloshed ashore

it was my grandfather who came from the west
coast of italy on a ship
refused to teach his wife or their children

his first language
the recipes his mother still prepared
he insisted his children
be american

maybe it was weeks on the ocean
its sound first a lullaby then
a thief
the constant rush and roar enveloping him
absolving him
of himself

how did you get here
hot caravan from the south
on a plane
to visit someone already here
by following
that long trail of paper
tests
signatures
ceremonies

maybe your family was
stolen
tortured
torn apart

my grandfather tried
to forget his country
i don't think he recognized luxury

i planted seeds
tomato and zucchini

so far two sprouts
zucchini i think

all week spring rain
the world is green and gray
our backyard is a small ocean of grass
patches where the green is darker
where it grows faster richer thicker
the grass grows so long it swirls
huge smooth swirls that look like they were painted

i don't know who it was
who came from scotland
but i visited the town with our name
wondered who it may have been
what they hoped to find
what they left behind

from the train
everything was blue green brown
blue sky green field brown hill
blue stream

the hills looked
so smooth alive
they looked like women
these women were planets
universes all their own
they create their own gravity pull you
a thread to their needle

we are born knowing
how to swim
do you remember

blue and green marbled
add sun
take a deep breath

everything oxidizes
loses its point
turns to rust
returns to the sea
begins again
blue green white

what about sorrow emptiness
how do you hold
emptiness under a microscope

can you unhear that first sea

blue brown green
veins of light through water
through marble
threads into fabric

threads into
us
a home
on land or sea

what color is oxygen gravity

do you remember
the small child maybe 3 years old in a yellow life vest

lifted from the too-full raft and passed
one pair of outstretched arms
to the next
his dark eyes vacant of everything

this
was his coming to america

or the boy inside the ambulance
his face all of him covered with dust
his whole world blew up
then came down
soft grey ash
and covered him
he lifted his small arm
touched his small hand to his head
and then
feeling the wetness in his hair
that ripple across his face

or the two year old in her pink sweatshirt
and tiny tennis shoes
howling at the uniformed man
who pats her mother down
maybe the mother tells herself to cooperate
keep it smooth
still thinking it will be better here
será mejor aquí

what is it
a child like these might steal

america has already been stolen

how did we get here

if there was a door
we could open inside our minds or
here on our chests
what country would we see inside

swimming lanes
are only divided on the surface

blue green white
history   the weaving and spooling of thread
stories wound round themselves
all of us get hungry all of us get tired
all of us sing the same song
with different words
around a maypole
a cotton field
a sea

blue green blue
and white
like mist
in san francisco
the family reunion
photograph of me and my children
in front of the stone wall
the wind so hard they couldn't open their eyes
behind us the bay
blue and white
the wind forcing the waves to bow

beyond that alcatraz
island of stone isolation

barbed wire
all our forms of entrapment

blue and green
white and brown
woven together
into history

behind us the sturdy universe
like a boat set sail for light
you know that light
shining through the blue green water
showing you blue green water

some smooth thread silk
another barbed wire
around and around
the story the vast oceans between us
they separate and connect us

do you remember
how to swim

at some point
we're all an island
a place too far
no one will survive the angry sea
we've wrapped around ourselves
thinking it's protection
no one will make it in to port
no one will comfort our lonely child

if you look out from any east coast
over the water
you'll see a west coast

each must learn
to use the elements available
earth sea sky
to make of life what we will
what we can
to weave loneliness
into silk into cotton
or a boat
learn to navigate by stars

the sky is a sea of stars
sometimes the dark eye of jupiter
swirling storm of anger
hurt or hate the same thing
consumes the sky the sea the earth
blue green white

imagine you're a three year old boy
crossing the enormous atlantic
  l'enorme atlantico
are you afraid excited
which parts of yourself do you
throw over which
slip
did he wonder will there be
someone to let me in
  ci sarà qualcuno che mi faccia entrare

it's all the same mind the same country
the same ocean weaving unweaving

a woman standing on an island
my dreams of making tomato sauce

what color is memory
this blue green
what is the sky but
all things
woven into a dress for the universe
pain turned to silk
universal dress for each of us to wear
while we stand while we sing
while we work and die

work hard we're told be rewarded
live comfortably
but each day becomes
work harder and longer
and harder and suffer
and suffer and suffer
until you disappear
          it doesn't make sense
you're ready
your feet are planted
you've positioned yourself
it's coming
you're prepared practiced
and then
          something else
you watch the light above
grow dim
others who haven't even paid attention
sail along above you
everything laid out before them like kings
you're sinking

water
growing colder
darker
then pressure
in your chest

there's no way to know
so you give your child to the boat
trade debt for the degree
give in and have the treatment

it's impossible to know
if it will work
if the side effects might be worse than the disease
if the side effects will
leave you drowning anyway
you might arrive and find all the doors locked

i once met a woman
from russia   she came with
her husband and son
both now dead her husband from
illness her son
here only a few months
delivering pizza
and
what do you say
he was killed by
an american disease
a gun poverty baltimore
he was shot for
what they thought was in
his empty pocket

this family came halfway round the world
to work hard
to make a better life
to lose a son

i don't know how she managed
how long it may have taken her
surely longer than it takes
to cross an ocean
drop by drop
    капля за каплей
surely longer than it takes
a boy to learn english

mile after mile after mile
nothing but h 2 and o
syllable by syllable
atom by atom
how far it is having a son
not having a son
имея сына
   не имея сына

there is no language for this
goodbye

sometimes you can't see the lighthouse
don't care that there may be a lighthouse
sometimes you are just too tired to lift your sunburned face
and look for the lighthouse
you're always supposed to believe
how do you believe

there is a lighthouse
which coast
did we sail from

how do you measure
what propels you
to give your child to the boat
the hot dry path
a country you've never seen
consider what it must be

a single molecule of water three atoms
that single person in a row boat
alone over the vast sea
azul зелёный bianca
two parents
how many more to make the boat the oar
the innumerable lives in the water beneath

finding

for the love of rhinos

it's all about being human
the music on the radio
symphonies poems
every book ever written
photograph taken lumps
of clay spun on wheels
even the coffees brewed
and handed to you by
a stranger calling your name

it's all practice   so
when you walk through
the zoo and see
the rhinos
standing snuffling
the green weeds in their
enclosure you also see
the precision
of their curved horns
how their ears
edged with delicate hairs
swivel toward sound and
then lay almost
hidden against
their necks

look at the lashes around their
prehistoric eyes the
softness in their grey
skin enclosing those impossible
bodies all the layers
of loneliness and earthly dust

dissecting light

from a high school anatomy text
i learned in latinate precision
to identify friends and enemies as if
dividing blood cells red from white
that light is seen and beyond seeing
that cutting something open
requires both pressure and gentleness
and reveals more than what's inside

how i studied that book and
its labels what comfort when
most everything in the world
is slippery to know
that every part of the body
has a name and a little black line
leading to it

for example your mastoid process
although it sounds like a disease is
actually a small flat bit of bone
protruding downward from
the end of your sternum
which generally speaking
protects your heart

one day a quiz tell the teacher
what you see under the microscope
the girl ahead of me who had
recently stolen my best friend
squinted into the microscope
shifted her weight squinted with

the other eye then looked
blankly up at our teacher
it was delicious a red
blood cell i knew
its shape a doughnut
with an indentation in the center
instead of a hole how delighted
i was when the teacher asked me to explain that to her

once i learned to see through
the safety goggles and ignore
the smell the dissections
not just frogs who are surprisingly
colorful inside i couldn't help
but wonder if humans are too
but a cat a fetal pig
a sheep's brain and
an ox's eye when i sliced
that eye open there were no
friends or enemies there was
beneath the jelly something
like a rainbow swirled on the dark retina
i scoured the diagrams
but found no line
leading to a delicate or muscular
word to identify these colors
the only answer my teacher said
it must be the last thing the ox saw
the last light that
entered its eye

the boy and the big white house

it might have been john or joe or gary
but i do remember
his white house on the corner
how big it was compared to mine
dark green hedges between it and the road
the way i couldn't look at it after
that august   he was
a teenager a few years older than i was then
it was said he'd
argued with his parents before
storming up to his room hanging
himself from his light fixture

i don't know what they fought over
what his parents' names were
or which one found him as they
went to call him for dinner or
to dole out his punishment or even to say
let's just put this behind us

i don't know how his mother pulled
his laundry from the dryer what
could she do with those clean socks
the stains on the knees of his
baseball uniform
that would never come out

sister

my sister would have had
my mother's dark hair and
brown eyes   i'm certain
she would have been determined
a block of a woman like out of
a giotto painting or trim and
feisty nearly invisible
except for her enormous personality
i'm not sure if she would be older
or younger or even a twin but she
would have liked the blue slurpee
better than the red   and she
would have talked more than
i did   she would have said
all the things i thought but kept
inside delicate glass
birds that would have shattered if
released and i would have loved
her for it   she would have pet every
dog we would have
met on our walks home from school
i would have stood a few feet
back watching her hands in all that
fur wishing i was free enough
to love things i did not know
clearly no reasonable person
can miss a sister who has
never existed   the laws of physics

insist that you cannot fill
an empty space you can not find
yet we know very well how to yearn
if you had never seen
a clear sky never
fallen into this girl's eyes would
you be distraught over
the lack of blue

one dance

it was never hard to know
which song to sing
even to strangers until you pulled me close
all i could do was look at you
behind your gray eyes again
for the first time
all the songs i ever knew drifted away
and because i could not sing
or even count in time i ran
flew away in my dad's buick
drove until i didn't recognize
mountains beneath sky
i stood on the edge of a thin road the car
resting behind me   tall grass and
dandelions swaying   the clouds were
too deep to see the sky and
it was all lightning in my mind
i replayed the silence the echo
of your arms around me how
long must i have stared at what i wanted
all the songs i might have sung
frozen on my tongue

finding

how many blades of grass before
we say *lawn* how many
grains of sand before *beach*
how much kindness
before *love*

it will not be found on a map
it is found
in not looking away
from the many greens
of trees the drip and rush
of rain the incessant beat
of thoughts the meeting of eyes

how human our need
for love and green   so many
maps yet i am lost
sun rises beyond the curtains
lines deepen on my face
long roads meander over
the skin of a drum

 what about the construction
of lives
the laying down of bricks words
bodies in love
i have been sitting here
cross-legged with my coffee
almost writing
for so long

see the poem in a painting
the sky always blue beyond clouds
sometimes a map is useless
you will be led by another compass
the way notes are magnetized to a song

the only thing to do

shimmering spider web
rippling plane of sunlight
the impossibility
of transmitting its precision
through words or a photograph

what do you do   turn
the clock back send yourself
a letter
maybe it's impossible
to be prepared for beauty

what is it
we think we know
what is knowing

maybe it's that first startle
when the sun reveals
the whole shape the measured
parallel lines the dew
dangling like jewels
the moment when everything
and time
has stopped

our thoughts shocked into
silence   it's only with so much
absence can you see
the perfect symmetry of web
its dark maker
precisely at its center and
you know you know
the only thing to do
is to see

everything depends on

the timetable directs me to the pier at
this hour and this minute so
i may pass along the waves
to you and what we might call ours
but everything depends on the anger in
the waves the downward
pressure of the clouds whether
or not the boatman's wife kissed
him before he left and if he had
his second cup of coffee   everything
depends on my favorite brown
hat remaining on my head on the
bridge we pass beneath continuing
to stand on your alarm
remembering to wake you
on the productivity of your own
coffee pot   everything depends
on the sun rising today on
the moon sacrificing its own face on
the tides created as the earth spins
on the tiny print of this
faded ferry schedule

time flickers

you hold a letter sent years ago
from your aunt
who died last week

in a dream someone presents
yellowed squares and rectangles
from a lover envelopes letters
cards warped from water

words you never received
sentences that have never
changed your eyes

you recognize the handwriting
wonder what those letters say
how you would have responded

you remember sitting together in a garden
you hear him speak in one language
and you respond in another

pointing at what i mean

honeysuckle blowing through my window
blossoms i ate with my grandmother

words that sprout along our tongues
but never bloom

poems also know
the unending length of longing

hands against a drum
are love

vines beneath and through
the dirt and years impossible memories

knowing we will die
and yet we do not talk

coffee stains appear
on paper beneath your mug

an arm of fern
uncurls toward river

the way we pretend
i end here you begin there

mirror neurons

two mimes facing each other
held together by an invisible force

their single movement
a form of human union

or the average man
lifting a car to free someone

or stopping to help a stranger
change a tire

observing someone in pain ignites the same part
of the brain as the one that blazes in the sufferer

twin lights whirling a communal nightmare
our neurons are ahead of us they fire

whether the one who suffers is friend or child or
stranger our neurons know

what we too often ignore
i have been too busy to mend the unraveling

coat of the old man who smells like pipe smoke
and lives in the shopping center

i have refused to abandon
the tangle of my own thoughts for

the mind required to hear another
even to my children's attempts to show me

how they can juggle then balance one ball atop a pyramid
you're in a team of two

your eyes are closed walking your partner guides you
one light hand on your shoulder stops you says

open your eyes and look in the mirror
through the window through the naked woods

a frosted lake you breathe in crystalline
details sense cold air beyond then

close your eyes a few more steps
open your eyes and look in the mirror

a vase of skillfully arranged flowers
each orange petal long green

stems you close your eyes take
a few dark steps   open your eyes

through this window an overflowing dumpster you
do this over and over around the room through the house

and you are amazed to find
yourself in everything

the last time open your eyes
and look in the mirror you face

another face its brain
slick and folded behind the forehead

hemispheres precisely divided
cells branching dendrites flashing

two eyes a nose
a mouth about to smile

a whole warm body something electric
and invisible between you

shimmer

it is a kind of tragedy the way we survive
pleasure the way we mourn the clear blue sky and
the company of love   it's always
the company of love she's after   even
in the form of strangers on a street   one day
she sits down in a shady spot and watches
the traffic and sun in late afternoon
and she sees is it love move all around her
even in the habits of traffic lights cars
honk and squeeze close people
gather at street corners their work
or school or children coming alongside
energy moves in rivers all around
coming from going in every direction
it's even in the sky as
the sun yawns between buildings
until darkness rises to hold those buildings and
that sky the people cars even the honking and traffic lights
until darkness is love come down like stars
and she survives that beauty everything
enjoyed and mourned everything even herself
shimmering with night

station

after li-young lee

your attention please
train number 7 alba's dream
destined for northern territory is now boarding

all ticketed passengers
please proceed to the gate marked *progress*

your attention please train number
yes we can bound for the road less travelled

and the high road is now departing
all ticketed passengers may board
between my ears

your attention please   train number 3 the twenty first century
has joined revolution after revolution
to become more guns than food

those who search for names
may inquire at their local government &
tragedy center or consult
their personal 8 balls

your attention please
words
dripping oozing like oil from large pores
support only artificial blooms

on what we thought was
the one tree of life

passengers with memories of hope
may board through many gates of despair

faithful members of the secret secret society
may proceed to their just reward at the feet of god

your attention please
under the pressure of your dream never close your eyes

there are no diamonds without coal

attention requires stillness followed by movement

tomorrow never keeps its appointments
you may not wait here

your attention please   train number 22
pained determination soon to be
exquisitely produced collects no dust
please leave your baggage backstage
behind the curtain labeled nothing real beyond this point

in some future the impossible may occur

you may board at any point of wonder

everything is a present

how to live

for alice herz sommers

picture a woman
three hours a day
at her piano playing
chopin schubert schuman
by heart   she is
one hundred and
eight years old   the skin
of her eyelids her hands is
soft alive   if you could
cup her cheek
in your palm
you'd be
amazed
how human she is

she says
music is food music
makes us happy   and
everything
is a present

in 1942 a younger woman said
goodbye
to her seventy-three-year-old
mother deported to a camp

in the camp a year later with
her husband and five-year-old son
she fed her fellow inmates

with the chopin
she memorized that motherless year
she gave them
more than a hundred concerts
transported them
she said *if only temporarily*

from hell

picture
skeletal prisoners
on folding chairs
energy
from their dark eyes
rising
with music
into the air

if we could photograph air
we'd see them rising
with the sound
rising and
drifting away

she and her son
remained
alive as long as she pleased
her jailors as long as she could
return them to
a self they recognized

she said
i look where it is
good   i know about the bad
but i look at the good

she had no
answer for
her son's questions
why do we have
no food   what
is a jew

instead she laughed
as she and her son
slept
for two years on the cold dirt

she said
where we can play
it can't be so bad
and
if the child
is near
the mother and the mother
smiles
the child smiles too

remember
everything
is
a present

another picture
she reclines on the grass her
small son sits beside her
somewhere beyond his
shoulders the sun
shines
both mother and son
laughing

our house

when her husband died
she had no choice but
learn to fly
she took the children left
the pantry stocked the perfume
he'd given her on the dresser
the fridge full of leftovers

without the family beneath
the roof collapsed strangers
broke locks and windows wires
were cut eaten through memories
drowned in puddles of rain

i listen as you tell
the story of this house
now twenty years later you restore it
find cans of green beans bottles of
hershey's syrup their lids
gnawed through the syrup licked
clean away the packet of
his letters above the linen cupboard
a lego house half destroyed or half
constructed a coffee mug proclaiming
grandma in bright red letters
one faded photo of the children standing
in a wading pool another
of them playing ball

you replace the roof haul away
the grit of squatters   tear

out the kitchen floor walls
everything
you sweep up shards of windows and
photo frames fallen ceilings and
insulation two decades of rodent droppings

i love this house   the scent
of saw dust and the current of that family
still pulsing here silvered
baby shoe on the mantle part of
a greeting card stuck to the floor its looping
cursive *hoping things are okay* and also
your passion for doing this because i imagine
this is our house
i smell our breakfast see us
each working in
a single sunlit room
later wine and a fire   and
this wild electricity
leaping from your body
into mine and back again a circuit
holding us in its charge

daisy with

being so
in love with you like
a daisy with the rain
i stretch roots
stem petals
i open
to the most beautiful
falling that lives
between us this
pulse
the sure sound
of rain loving ground
raindrops on
petals skin
i open take you in
all of me glistening

feared loss

after only one night
staying in her half of the new apartment
hissing across our bed at the other cat
she is gone

we call crawl into every corner
check every closet under every table
for my only cat
closest thing i have to a child
not even to hear a small fearful meow

we wonder if it was the open door
if she ran down the stairs into the apartment below
or worse
out into the street

i'm out the door calling
looking under every parked car
both sides of the street
asking new neighbors
wiping my tears
i describe her tortoise shell stripes
her white belly and paws

i blow my nose
imagining she was hit
tortured by neighborhood children
or has fallen down a gutter and is being eaten by rats

i even walk the alley
praying for anyone who has ever lost a child
remembering the ones i lost

the sudden strangeness in my body
two weeks late and somehow taken over
until i felt sick

there was pain and blood
and later i learned that it was you
my first child come to visit
and leave
your brother or sister more persistent
stayed a whole six weeks
until i collapsed

then years of crying
imagined childless birthday parties
useless concerns about school day care
what your father would think

others have lost whole complete children
named and known them
snatched from playgrounds or their own beds
how do we do it
go on without

i walk past fallen down shacks
garages given up to gravity
once content with cars
now full of stained mattresses shattered mirrors
used syringes and discarded packaging
i would not want you to see this
be here in this kind of pain

i call their names
asking god and st anthony
like my mother taught me
to bring them all back
my children my cat everyone else's too
i want them all back

in tongues

all night we've been reading
poems to each other
all night i've listened to his sound
watched his mouth make words

soon he will be my husband
our children are carried
sleeping quietly inside him
like language he doesn't know he has yet

waiting for what he calls
the right time when i imagine
they will come dancing in and out of me

and teach us how to speak
he says *good morning sweetheart*
i know he's talking to the cat
but i hear him wake our daughter

highway 101

our first week married
we drove
south from portland
along the coast
toward california

i remember the road
winding in places
sitting beside you in the rented car
the sense of hours of road ahead

in california we took
pictures of each other
beside the ancient trees
we looked so small so
inconsequential framed
in the viewfinder now

i see you twelve and a half
years later sitting up
in bed your back to the window
moonlight so much moonlight
through the open curtain

and it's highway 101 a full moon
on the pacific everything blue-black
bright white or sparkling
somewhere between

we passed cities farms and
cabins built into the cliffside
designed to withstand

wind erosion time i wondered
what life would be like there to wake
season after season together
beside the ocean toast and
raspberry jam coffee to go with
the fog and maybe a walk
on the beach before we sit to work

we even visited the sea lions saw
their huge bodies on the rock ledge
the inside of the cave where they
winter it was the first time
i'd seen sea lions their immenseness
more like elephants than lions
almost covering the rock

from the highway at one point i saw
so briefly the most beautiful
sand dunes everything
golden the shapes
indescribable the curves of women
too beautiful to exist

you drove us to haystack rock
described your childhood visits as i
enjoyed an ice cream something
the shop called french silk
a combination of several
kinds of chocolate
to me so much paradise

we walked me licking you talking
and i thought of the highway the
way it runs so close to the edge

sometimes of the fog that
blinds but mostly of all that
space we planned to cover
all the hours together in what
might feel like
a too-small car and
out of all that i might have feared what
i remember was
my sense of relief
to be beside you

it was the first time i'd seen the west my first time
as a wife your wife and my husband
also a poet we stopped to photograph

lighthouses tidal pools the rocks and their
barnacles sea grasses waving
orange starfish relaxing their
legs thrown over each other

we passed the one good camera
between us every few minutes careful
not to drop the precious thing it was all
these years later i can't tell which pictures
were yours which mine

night poem to my husband

after billy collins

i get up from the tangled bed and go outside
a bear leaving its cave
a hermit crab looking for its next shell

only to stand on the lawn
a simple person
amid sleeping brick houses

if i were younger i might be thinking
about my newest lover
his cologne

or the smoke in my favorite sweater
but as it is i am simply aware
someone standing in the grass

sensing only the cold wetness
of the grass and the breeze
that stirs the tops of the trees

the cat has followed me out
and stands a little behind
her eyes lifted as if she were wondering

what i am doing
what are those lights in the sky
and there was something else i wanted to tell you

something about the fresh peach comfort
we share in our house
but now i am wondering if you are even listening

and why i bother to tell you these things
that will never make a difference
unfinished sentences crunched up leaves

but this is all i want to do
tell you that down the alley
a few rabbits were running

the sky was clear and high above me
and that at one point the moon
looking like a freshly peeled orange

our girl would like to eat
appeared quite clearly
from behind a thin cloud

learning the names

in the grocery store my girl
points to a bunch of pink
carnations in cellophane and asks
if we can buy those roses i know
learning the names of things
is difficult things like *carnation*
rose and more complex
words with layers like petals
wound tightly round each other petals
reaching away words like *mommy*
daddy brother surprise

what should i call it when she squeezes
the baby's hand as he reaches for
something she doesn't want him
to have or when his blue eyes shine
up at mine until she elbows him
off my leg or when she steps
hard on his fingers and what do i call it

when i just want to drive
away and i imagine the silent
apartment the uncluttered
floor i'd walk every day after
my shower before or after the coffee
i'd sip next to a sunny
window in glorious
loneliness

i forget to explain
the difference between carnations
and roses and the too small chance
that daddy will bring either
home as a surprise so we
buy them ourselves take them
home and fistfull the blossoms
apart dropping them petal by petal

my love

all i can be is
thankful to be caught
in the rain to have the day
washed from us
to be left glistening
walking our children through
the cemetery across from our house
it has begun to rain i have
no umbrella just a large
stroller for our infant son
and our three year old
who wants to be home
who wants to know
that statue's name *that girl mommy*
the one with the lamb she's in
the bushes on a cement platform
nearly surrounded by bushes with new
green leaves mary is kneeling arms
outstretched to a lamb and three stone children
is she their mommy this
climbing through the bushes onto the platform
look someone gave her flowers

we're walking to the pond
in the cemetery to feed the fish
these breadcrumbs the grass
has started growing again
the sky is full and gray

today four boys stand
on the rocks around the pond

re-baiting their lines and throwing them out
they do not look up at us there's
no room among the stories
they're threading

after two handfuls of bread and no sign
of fish or geese our toddler
wants to go into the gazebo
to watch the big boys fish
and the raindrops bounce on the pond

we have been walking over
our neighbors the dead and
although i apologize every time
they have not responded perhaps
it is better this way i would
not know how to explain
to our child who looks like me
our baby who looks like you

my love i've been walking
in the cemetery across from our house
the sun has risen the grass is growing
and the bushes have new leaves
our little one is throwing bread crumbs
to the animals in the rain mary is watching
with her lamb we're coming home
glistening with rain

purity

after she refused
to take a nap
screamed and stomped

for forty minutes woke
her little brother snatched
the blue train from his hand

and flung it to the floor
where i was sure to
trample it hurting my foot

hurting the train i'm asking
myself if i'd known it would feel
like this would i have chosen

this then my girl
asks for a banana whole
and peeled and in her hand

and a glass of cold milk
all i can see is
the banana's

golden whiteness as she
raises it to her mouth
takes a bite

the milk's blue whiteness
sloshing in her cup
and i remember

the sweetness and coldness
she's tasting the way
everything is mixed

addition subtraction division

across from our house
parkwood cemetery where we
like to walk in spring and fall

today it's january almost
cold enough to snow the christmas
greens have faded or fallen

sideways in the wind the once-bright
red ribbons have given up their glow
walking through i read

the names smith schmidt clark
diangelo as the three of us meander
toward the pond and the wooden gazebo

the plaque tells me again it's
provided for our comfort
in the name of a son who

passed at only 23
i worry how his parents
managed those first few hours

days and months without him
while my child pulls chocolates
from her pocket

divides them for us to share
she will be eleven next week
her brother is recently eight

i wonder what it is i really want
to say to them as we tell him how we
used to bring picnics here

when he was very small just
to be somewhere not home
he says he doesn't remember unwraps

a green foiled chocolate then
a red all of them from the half off
bag i bought last week

i wonder about my friend who never told me about
his cancer and the frozen blue day
we left him in the ground

my daughter says she saw
the graves of children near the entrance
a baby a three year old a twenty year old

i wish her not to be among such a group
as she and her brother call to the geese
who live here the wind blows

i'm cold even in my wool coat
even after my chocolates i say
i want to go home they

object as we take the long way
past stone markers indicating beloved
wife husband mother father

daughter son small planted
christmas trees the occasional
windstrewn scarecrow from an autumn arrangement

a canopy and wooden panels laid down
small protections from glaring sun sticky mud
dark things a family might carry back

view from my sofa

after alex grant

i slip in between abandoned toys and heaps of laundry
to be folded while my children advise each other

on how to defeat the flame-red monster in the video
game on tv its and their cries fill the room

echo through the house i drop my expectations
what might be accomplished today pick up

my now cold coffee and too-soft cheerios it's
spring break a whole week of goals given up

i repeat a buddhist prayer the five
remembrances *i am sure to become old i am*

sure to become ill i am sure to die i am sure
to become separated from all that is dear to me i am

the owner and heir of my actions i get up
to reheat my coffee again and think

of my husband of those girlhood jump rope games of the way
veins on grandmother's hands popped back after i flattened them

i sip hot coffee watch robins flutter from the backyard into air

becoming old

a body is only as strong as
its weakest cell

today my cells are saying
enough today
i've become old time
to reconsider

it was scary looking back
at just last week the thoughts
it would be so much easier to
or not to

or silence
sometimes it solves
everything
sometimes
darkness

today
i'm soaking in the tub
writing this poem
in a small journal do you
remember those simple elements
paper pen
my back aches so i change position

this morning i was excited
to remember our pharmacy
gave my husband seven
pills a week's supply unless
you're waiting for approval

our first child is turning sixteen
my mind goes back
to the snow we drove home in
three now
instead of two the way
we felt terrified
and competent dear god

but now in my neighborhood
of the northern hemisphere
flannel is inappropriate
in february we watch chunks
of glaciers the size of manhattan
crumble into the sea scientists
watch and film their voices
nothing but awe

in the bathtub
i feel the heat
rise and escape
the water the pleasure
of these simple elements
heat water skin

someone on tv
said something about sylvia no
something about
an oven a gas oven
like ours i'm the one
who thought of sylvia

today my cells are
telling me we are old
we cannot see clearly
afraid of how many
more days there may be
disproportionately
thankful for a hot bath
a small round pill
a glass of cool water

bra shopping

in the mirror
below my right shoulder blade
something not
familiar not
me

a dot
not a freckle
maybe dark blue
another
inches away

they're
tattoos

three years ago
they drew on me
something like
a sharpie
angles the doctor provided
guides for radiation
my body abstract art
and target

their spotless voices said
the marker will wear off
but these tattoos
they're so small
you'll never notice them

and it was done
sharp points
place their ink

there was no
while you're here today
do you understand
are you ready

they
made their marks
marks i can see
marks that will remain
as long as i do

the poster

just under 8 feet tall
it stood in one of the huge windows
of the library's main branch
designed and created
to advertise an evening
of poetry and conversation
with two married couples
all four poets
two friends and us

that evening
i had my picture taken
in front of the window
with the poster but that image
isn't something i can touch
it's lost floating
in dark digitized ether

i was proud of myself
of us the main branch
of the library in baltimore
where i grew up a huge poster
of this quiet
little poet and her husband
and two friends the picture
of me was taken by your nephew
at a family reunion it appears
on the back of my first book
the photo of you i took
on a walk around lake roland

with our family it appears
on the back of your first book

i asked the librarian
even though
you thought i was crazy
too big
even for the top of our car
i had to ask friends for help

our house too cozy for
a library or office it leans
against a wall in our dining room
the children and you
still tease ask *why*
i say *why not*

but
it's not a question
all those poem-less
years for time
away from words
when we're mom and dad
workers brother husband
wife patient and caregiver

and if we live long enough
to begin to forget
everything
and then

go on forgetting
there it will be images of ourselves
our names the date in huge font
in our dining room
for all the times we have
and may need to be
reminded of ourselves

while you were sleeping

i took out the trash   i took
that trip i've been wishing for
that extraordinary place where
none of the food
looks like food at least none
we've ever had
while you were sleeping
i plucked all my gray twice
as many grew back
while you were sleeping
i borrowed your body
i took it for a walk and enjoyed
being taller for a while but
the clouds were more alarming than
i had expected   it's very easy
to get lost when everything is
cold white mist   like
a dream except you can still
stub your toes and whack
your shins   while you
were sleeping i dug
and planted and weeded
a garden   the dirt the soil
was thankful joyful the ground
was glad to be useful   look
at those jubilant tomatoes
while you were sleeping i managed
to clean the kitchen   it was
perfect everything shiny and
in its place for the space
of a breath

while you were sleeping
i watched you sleep and dream
i watched your chest and the way
it lives without you i watched your eyes
and wondered what they saw beneath
their lids   while you
were sleeping i waited for you
to wake   i wondered if you
would still be you if you
would find me still me

the other side of the world

when we wake it is evening there
we smell coffee and move
in its direction   they have
already done their dinner dishes
we make lists they count
accomplishments
day is nearly done with them
kites that might have flown
have been flown   children
who learned to crawl or walk
or read have done so   their parents
are thrilled and terrified today
and for years to come   dishes
that were to be dropped
have shattered and been swept away
those who were to leave us
have done so   families
mourn or will soon all of us
cool as the sun goes down
birds fire or the grave
wait for what is left

imagist marriage

so many years
a man and woman
have passed
in this old house
their favorite spot
the big front porch that
wraps around all spindles
and railings oversized
ferns or red begonias where
they sit
side by side
nothing
but a small table between them
two nearly empty glasses
and all those years swirling in the air

dreams of the future

one evening i return
to find my children grown
they don't need me
to make their food
wash their clothes read
their books aloud
i stand in the living room and wonder

one evening i return
to find my husband
an old man in a chair
too large for him
i look down at the lines on my hands then
for a window to use as a mirror

one evening i return
to find my home a forest
trees instead of sofa
stars instead of ceiling
i sit down and watch until
the sun shows herself
then pull the fallen leaves
around me and sleep

Acknowledgements

Thanks to the editors of the following journals in which these poems appeared in slightly different forms:

In Tongues, Dancing Shadow Review, Vol. 3, Number 1, 1996

Feared Loss, Baltimore Review, Summer Issue, 1997

Thoughts on Making Soup and War, The Mas Tequila Review, Issue #1, 2010, *Touch*, Finishing Line Press, 2011

Going to Bed after PBS, Gargoyle 51, 2006, *Touch*, Finishing Line Press, 2011

Night Poem to my Husband, *Touch*, Finishing Line Press, 2011

Learning the Names, *Touch*, Finishing Line Press, 2011

Purity, *Touch*, Finishing Line Press, 2011

About the Author

Virginia Crawford, long-time teaching artist with the Maryland State Arts Council's Artists-in-Education program, has co-edited two anthologies: Poetry Baltimore: poems about a city, and Voices Fly, An Anthology of Exercises and Poems from the Maryland State Arts Council's Artist-in-Residence Program published by CityLit Press. She earned degrees in Creative Writing from Emerson College and the University of St. Andrews. Her book Touch was published in 2011 by Finishing Line Press. She lives in Baltimore.

Apprentice
House Press
Loyola University Maryland

Apprentice House is the country's only campus-based, student-staffed book publishing company. Directed by professors and industry professionals, it is a nonprofit activity of the Communication Department at Loyola University Maryland.

Using state-of-the-art technology and an experiential learning model of education, Apprentice House publishes books in untraditional ways. This dual responsibility as publishers and educators creates an unprecedented collaborative environment among faculty and students, while teaching tomorrow's editors, designers, and marketers.

Outside of class, progress on book projects is carried forth by the AH Book Publishing Club, a co-curricular campus organization supported by Loyola University Maryland's Office of Student Activities.

Eclectic and provocative, Apprentice House titles intend to entertain as well as spark dialogue on a variety of topics. Financial contributions to sustain the press's work are welcomed. Contributions are tax deductible to the fullest extent allowed by the IRS.

To learn more about Apprentice House books or to obtain submission guidelines, please visit www.apprenticehouse.com.

Apprentice House
Communication Department
Loyola University Maryland
4501 N. Charles Street
Baltimore, MD 21210
Ph: 410-617-5265
info@apprenticehouse.com • www.apprenticehouse.com

www.ingramcontent.com/pod-product-compliance
Lightning Source LLC
LaVergne TN
LVHW051422080426
835508LV00022B/3197